OUT OF SYNC

A Collection of Poems

HIROSH BHASKAR

BookLeaf Publishing

India | USA | UK

Dedication

To a group of people who strongly believe
that I do have the literary spark

A thought that I seriously suspect is
misplaced, when I am really such a lark

Preface

This is a collection penned down whenever the urge comes to capture a feeling or suddenly when a situation crops up, which requires one's inner self to put it down in words. The collection can be termed more as rhythmic prose than poetry in its true sense. The writing is of a rambling nature and not set to any metre or any other such things required as per the science of writing poems.

Sunday Musings

A lazy Sunday morning
The weather overcast and raining
My dear away in a retreat
Giving herself a treat
On a sofa, I plonked down
Looking at the drizzling rain
A hot cup of coffee
By my side
And the morning papers
In front of me
Ready for a long
Session of gorging
On news cooked up
And fake

Contrived by devious minds
Focused on ratings
Fuelling friction
With lies and half truths
Creating sensation
With anything
And everything
Celebrating
Others' failure and misery
Taking a sip of my coffee
Sublime
I had just got into it
Gleaning the headlines
That I felt a presence
Left and right
On my shoulders
Firmly holding to my ears
Getting my complete
Attention immediately
'Who are you guys
Crash landing like this
Disturbing my solitude
Without a semblance
Of courtesy
Or a prior notice

Surprising me like this'
'I am your conscience'
Said the one on my right
'I am your well-wisher'
Said the one on my left
'And we have the right
To crash land on you'
both chorused
'What do you want'
My irritation evident
I asked them
'Leave me alone
Can't you see
That it is a Sunday
And I want no company
After a long time
I am getting some me time'
'I know what you mean'
said the well-wisher
Firmly perched on my left
Bellowing into my ears
Pulling on his cigars
'I am here to help you
Against that prude guy
Perched on your right

Beware of him and his advice
As he is out to disturb your peace'
'Shut up', said the conscience
On my right
'He has to be up on his feet
Has promises to be kept
Things to do
And no time to while away
Reading Worthless news
Of things that never happened
Concocted by fertile minds
With no concern about its impact
Sprouting public interest
And flouting it ad nauseam
Get up you and be about
You have only one day
And lots of things to do'
I looked at him wearily
Thinking that why this guy
Can't take leave on a Sunday
And leave us alone
To indulge in what we like
'Don't listen to him'
Said my well-wisher
Pulling on his cigar

'See me, this day is to relax
So ignore that prude and rela...aax'
He drawled, taking another
Pull on his cigar
Winking at me while doing so
I liked this guy
I warmed up to him
A kindred heart
doing his job right
That is, being my well-wisher
To the hilt
The one on my right
Has now started a tap dance
Chanting in my ears
'Get up, Get up, Ohoy, Ohoy'
Rat a Tat, he created a racket
Competing with the rain outside
Which by now has become
A torrential storm
'Hey, stop that racket', I said
My mood, by now, spoiled
'Why should I get up now'
'You have a lot to do
Timelines to be met
Promises made to be kept

You are already late
Get up and put together
Your breakfast first'
'Ha! Ha! Ha'! my well-wisher roared
'Putting together a breakfast indeed
Who does that on a Sunday
When you can have it at leisure
From a good restaurant'
This chattering between the
Left and the right
Was getting on my nerves
And I wanted to pack off
Both these guys
What conscience told
Was on the back of my mind
And I knew that I had
A lot to do
Which I cannot accomplish
Being on my back
So with utmost reluctance
I pulled my posterior
From the sofa with which
It has become bonhomie with
'You will regret this'
Said my well-wisher

And I had also no doubt about it
But I had decided to go with my conscience
To do the jobs
My procrastination had piled up
'Off with you guys, I have work to do
Let me put my hands to good use
Starting off with a breakfast
which may turn into a brunch'
'Awww', said the one on my left
'Awww', said the one on my right
'Now don't you two gang up against me
Give me some Peace
As I am going to play with fire'.

Adieu

One's final adieu
Is it relief
Is it a loss
Is it a passage
To nether life
Or the end in itself
From pleasure
Pain, sorrow and fear
The heat and the cold
When your worldly body
Is shed, cremated or buried
How does one enjoy
The pleasures assured in Heaven
Or the travails threatened in Hell

Without a body
To feel the pleasure or pain
Can anyone hurt
An ethereal thing
That we call a soul
By bodily harm
By scalding oil
Can it traverse
The string across the fire
Or all this can be safely assumed
Creation of a devious mind
Limited by imagination
To contain masses
By threat of retribution
And the offer of Heaven
As corruption for adherence
To Archaic beliefs
Professed by our religions
Each trying to surpass the other
To be the sure shot way
The best travel agent
To your nether world.
Make good of what you got now
And let the unknown remain unknown.

Unleased

Caged in concrete
Against my will
I waited aeons
Pounding restlessly
On the walls
Relentlessly
Looking for a breach
Praying to nature
For strength
And support
At last, it came
In unabated measure
As torrential rain
I pushed and pulled
With added vigour
Provided by nature
Totally impatient
In my confinement

Finally, they had to relent
And open the gates
Freeing me from the dungeon
I rushed forth in all my vigour
Devouring everything
In my path
That man built
Without a care
Fledging my muscles
Aching for a tussle
Charting my own course
Avoiding the path trodden
Racing on in exhilaration
To my Mon Amour
Who has been pining for me
Waiting to embrace me
With open arms
And I raced
Comforted
In my knowledge
That the Lord is with me!!!!!!

Office Pangs

Working on deadline
Looking line by line
Searching in the myriad
Fact and figures
For solution and salvation
Without a break
Without a rest
Trudging on
Till the end
I raised my eyes
From the blinking screen
And looked outside
To focus my eyes
On something green
For some respite
From the pain in my eyes

And was surprised to find
That the rain had gone
And the setting sun
Has painted the sky
In all its splendour
Clouds mauve and pink
Floating in rainbow hues
I pushed myself up
From where I was entrenched
Hit the buttons, shut down my lap
My feet moving outside
On their own volition
Towards the mystic beauty that enchanted
me
It started to drizzle again
The natural display still on
And I walked on
Enjoying the spray of water
On my face, cooling my eyes
Slowly getting drenched
Without a care in this world
And then it crossed my mind
Oh my goodness, what a pity
I missed all this, being a nutty
Cooped up in my office

However air conditioned it was
Bent over some MIS data
For which nobody cared
When I could be here, outside
Living the life as it should be
What for was I toiling my heart out
When I could have a reasonable life
With what I have
And that it was time
To come out of the rut
That I have gotten into
 It is better to have
A body stout
A healthy heart
To look back
On memories sweet
Of time well spent
Of good deeds done
And friends to care
And share
The things that you hold close
Than to toil
And boil
For an end
In a golden tomb.

Hats

Multiple hats one has to don
Whether it suits one or not
With or without one's choice
Define one's attitude to the world
So it is better to wear with elan
With gusto, with confidence
Ignoring the strange looks
Thrown at you askance
By public, near and dear
Posing as the know-all well-wisher
For you yourself are your
Best and worst critic
Answerable to none.

Footprints

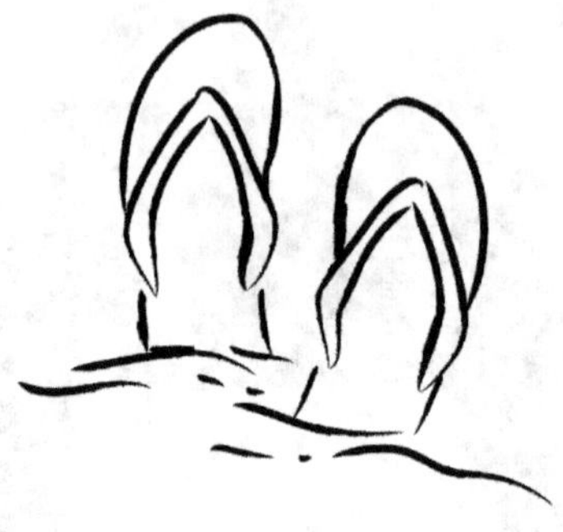

Footprints in the sand
Going round and round
Hither and thither
Without any care
Directionless
Clueless
To be erased
By the blowing wind
Or by the tide
From the face of this earth
Forever like in death

Soliloquy

Prostate on my back
The ceiling in my sight
Painted pristine white
A very ordinary sight
From any hospital bed
Immobile as one can be
Emulating savasana
Of an accomplished yogi
Which was rather easy for me
As not a muscle moved
In my body even if I willed
Or if it did want to move
On its own volition

I lay here on my back
Looking at the ceiling
My thoughts.............
The only moving thing
Which had the speed of lightning
Going back and forth
Like a pendulum
Swinging from reality to fantasy
From what could have been
To what it has become

I have been here on my back
Looking at the ceiling
For what seemed
Like an eternity
As I have lost the ability
To look anywhere else
Rooted to this bed
By a tube through my throat
And a tube through my nose
And tubes through god knows where else
My body abused
Beyond one's imagination
Trussed up, probed and handled

Like a guinea pig
On an experiment table

I lay here on my back
Looking at the ceiling
Not knowing to despair
Or hope
Not able to believe
The reassurances
Covered in endearments
Of my near and dears
Who made a beeline
To where I lay
Every day
Day by day
Their reassurances could not remove
The dread instilled in me
From the details drummed up by me
On my laptop searching on Google
Of the affliction implied
By my doctor with a look on his face
Indelibly imprinted on my mind
I know the reassurances
Of my friends and relatives
Were more for themselves

Than for me
As they also could not accept
The writing on the wall

I lay here on my back
Looking at the ceiling
Regretting the lifestyle I led
Of not making better use
Of the precious time
When I had it in hand
Wasting it on mundane things
Procrastinating leisure
In my effort to push my career
Which now I know
Have little value
When you weigh it with
Time that should have been
Well spent on
Things we love
With our nears and dears
Travels that I wish I made
To places that I dreamt off
I really can't imagine
Why I had put it off
When many had cajoled me

To find a little time
For things other than
One's job and career
I was obstinate
And my priorities lopsided
I thought that I had
All the time in the world
Never expecting that
It would be cut off
Like this in my prime
Oh! What I would give
To go back in time
And do things differently
If provided the opportunity

I lay here on my back
Looking at the ceiling
A prisoner in my body
Slowly shutting down
Like a person
Who drank Socrates poison
Awaiting the day of deliverance
From this world to nether world
From my trials and tribulations
For I know in my heart

That there is no light
At the end of this tunnel
But a fight I will put
Till my last breath.

Corrupt

Thou are corrupt
Said the politician to the bureaucrat
Who looked back askance
And said
Hi,... it is like
Pot calling the kettle
Black
To know what is corrupt
Just look in the mirror
And know the fallacy
In calling me corrupt
When you are corrupt
To the core
Corrupting everything

That you touch
Corrupting the youth
Corrupting the system
Poisoning the mind
By feeding disinformation
Corrupting for power
Corrupting for pelf
Distorting the truth
Couching it in half truth
Disturbing the peace
As your tribe trive
In unrest and turbulence.
Taken aback
The politician retorted
You have no right
To talk back like that
Yours is to listen and obey
And get things done
As per my whims and fancy
For the people have gave
Me the right through their vote
I am their elected representative
And I act on their behalf
Whatever I do
They have endorsed

And my every action
Is for their good
The bureaucrat laughed
We are both public servants
You for the short haul
And I for the long haul
Your term will end in 5 years
I will be here for years and years
So be careful in what you do
As you will have to go
Back
To the public
For an encore
While I don't need
Anything of that sort
To continue here
The politician, unperturbed, said
Public has short memory
And we are adept
At manipulating it
When it is required
A controversy
A religious conflict
A sentimental story
Of sacrifices made

Irrespective of it
Being true or false
Is all that is needed
To set things right
They will lap
All that we feed
Root for us
And bring us back
So you better do
What I say
Or be prepared
For a place in hell
As it is a certain
What your life will become
If things do not go
As per my wish
And you will wish
That it is better
To be in hell.

Politician

Switching sides,
One wonders why,
Personal gains,
Their hearts' desire,
Ideologies
That public desire
Just a tired fire.

With words blithe
They deceive,
Their conscience,

They readily leave,
Principles,
Like autumn leaves,
Is shed as selfishness breathes.

Their loyalty
A fleeting dream
As power and wealth,
Their souls redeem,
They jump the ship
With nimble feet,
And public thought
Always at their feet

Their voters,
Their supporters
Bewildered
And dismayed,
Their values slayed
But still, they vote,
With hopeful eyes,
For changes,
That never truly rise.

Getting Grounded

In the banking hall,
He once held sway,
A manager stern,
In his working day.
No nonsense tolerated,
Putting all in line,
Now retired,
He is in line
In the same banking hall

He seeks correction,
A pension plight,
Error found in pension,
Justice in sight.
But staff, like timber
Ignore his face,
Just another number
In the queue's space.

He clears his throat,
Looks right and left
For a familiar face
Nobody looks at him
Eyes glued
To the screen in front
Ignoring the guy in front
With indignation bold,
'Attend to me'! He unfolds.
But youthful clerks,
With eyes aglow,
Tap screens,
Oblivious to his
'Hey, you know'!

Their automated smiles,
A distant hum,
'Sir, please wait',
The robotic drum.
He taps his cane,
With growing ire,
'Didn't I run this branch
With heart and fire'?

A front office clerk
With a frozen stare,
Asks for his ID,
Without a care.
He hands it over,
With disdain so fine,
'Don't you know me?
I made this bank shine'!

After long hours
Of running from
Pillar to post
His pension fixed,
He takes his leave,
With warnings given,
None to receive.
He exits, shaking head
In dismay,
'Banking's lost its soul,
Gone astray'!
Now it is run by robots
For people like robots
'Oh my', those were the days
When I was at the helm
What a feeling it was

When Everyone jumps up
The moment I step in

Now no respect
Everybody indifferent
Am I not the person same
Why don't they give credence
Said he
Forgetting the age
Old adage
That once retired
You get grounded

Trigger

Sunset's warmth
Upon my skin,
Echoes of memories
Locked within,
The waves caress
The shore once more,
A familiar serenade
I adore.

In this haven,
It felt like heaven
Where laughter echoed,
Never to part,

The horizon stretch
Far and wide,
A canvas of moments,
Side by side.

Relics of youth,
Seashells bright,
Reminds me of joy,
Of endless nights,
The salty scent,
The ocean's roar,
Floods my soul,
Forever more.

I breathe the air,
Thick with the past,
Memories well up,
Of playful deeds
Of joyful nights
Spent with friends

Longing to relive,
To reprise,
Moments lost,
Yet forever wise.

The distant horizon
Triggers me,
To revisit those days
Of wild ecstasy,
In this sacred space,
I find my peace,
Where sweetness of love,
Laughter and memories
Remain at touching distance

Testing Limits

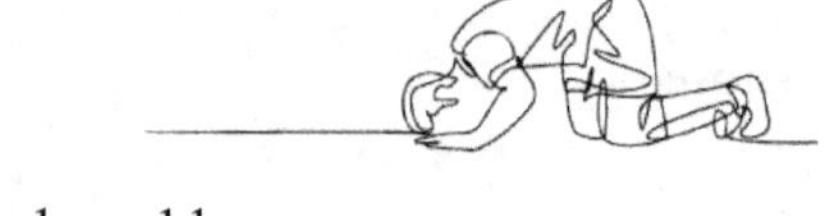

Weathered boots
Worn with pride
Echoes of triumphs
Deep inside
Trophies gathered
Battles won
Moments cherished
Forever done.

In stadiums loud,
That shone so bright,
Crowds chanting
On nostalgic nights,
From seaside greens
To mountain grounds
My feet danced in trance
With victorious rounds.

The roar of fans
A deafening sound,
Adrenaline rushed

My heart unbound,
From dusty fields
To lush estates
My passion burned
Through sweat and fate.

Now twilight beckons
Shadows fall
My body tested
But spirit tall,
Though pace has slowed
Heart desires
To chase the dream
Through lingering pain.

If time permits
Once more I will don
The Super Venom boots
Gifted by an enamoured fan
I'd test the greens
And score again
But age yields wisdom
Not lost zeal,
My love for football
Forever real.

Until my legs
No longer can,
I'll play on,
Beneath the golden pan,
For every pass
Every goal
Every cheer
Every teammate
Who shared with me
The high and the fame
Is etched in memory
Forever clear.

Inner Peace

In twilight's hush,
Where petals sway,
A secret haven
Awakens to stay,
A tapestry rich
With colours bright,
A marvellous sight
In morning's delight.

The garden's heart
Beats strong and free,
Lotus pond's calm
A soothing sight to see,
Birds flit and flutter
A whirling storm
Drinking in sweetness
From the blooming flowers

Hummingbirds hover,
Iridescent sheen
Magpies and sparrows
A chorus serene,
Butterflies dance,
Dragonflies play,
As the gentle breeze
Calms your sense

In the front courtyard
I sit and unwind,
The garden's beauty
A sight so pretty
The world slows its pace
As I breathe and sigh
In harmony with nature
The clouds drifting by.

In this haven of peace
I while away my time
Retirement's golden days
In a sunny way
Potting and planting,
Nurturing with care,

Watching life flourish,
Without a single snare.

This garden of wonder
A treasure so rare
A symphony of life
Beyond compare
A place to call home
Where love resides
A serene escape
From worldly woes.

All Is Fair

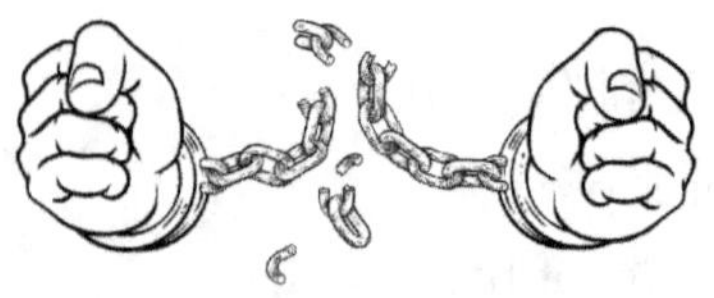

A politico so sly and fine
Spent a lot of money
Bribed clergy in line.
Promised the moon
And stars up high
Things he never meant to try.

He primed the people
With vows so grand
But his opponent
A newcomer, took his stand
With fresh ideas
And an honest face,
The newcomer won
The election's pace.

The politico's jaw
Dropped to the floor,
His plans foiled

His cash spent galore.
He learned that day
With a sad, sad grin,
Money can't buy wins,
And lies won't spin

I am sorry to say
That above is a tale fairy
That one will never pass by
But one can always daydream
That people will see through the game
Someday and will have power
to bring change whatever

No Second Chance

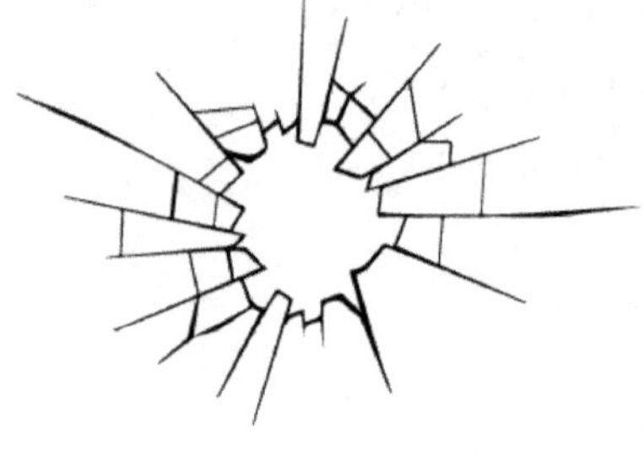

A fleeting dream
A fatal night
A celebration cut short
A future lost in light
No helmet to shield
No caution to guide
A bike with three
A risk they couldn't hide

The screen faded black
The movie unwatched
As death's dark whisper
A young soul clutch
The parents' anguish
A grief so true
A child lost, a future,
One can never renew

Friends mourn in shock
In pain and in tears
Memories of laughter
Echo in their ears
What could've been,
What should've been
Regrets remain
Under the setting sun

Society's loss
A talent, a beam
A kindred soul
A light extinguished
A heart that ceased
No second chance
No turning back time
A young life silenced
A memory, forever aligned

In sorrow, we gather
To bid farewell
To a life unlived
A story, others will tell
May her memory live

May her soul rest free
As those who survive
Are forced to live on
Burdened with the thoughts
Of what it might have been
Had they a second chance.

Place Of Worship

Hallowed halls
Of reverence stand
Testaments to faith
Or so it's planned
But do they serve
The divine
Or mortal might
Are they bastions
Of hope
Or instruments
Of control of the mind

Were they built
To bring solace
To the soul
Or to exert power
By the master

Were they built
To control the masses
Or did they rise
From a desire to unite
Or were they crafted
To manipulate
To ignite

In the depths of history
A complex web is spun
Of societal identity
Of power
Of everyone
A paradox unfolds
Of purpose and design
As institutions evolve
Their roles entwine.

Do they provide
A sanctuary
A refuge
From life's strife
Or have they become
Mere facades
A lucrative rife

In developed lands
Churches crumble
Or transform
Into commercial hubs
 Where Mammon's the norm.

Yet, in developing realms
Religion's a thriving trade
Superstition's a currency
That's eagerly displayed
A paradox indeed,
Where Faith's a double-edged sword
Bringing hope to some
While others are
Exploited
Ignored.

What's the future
For these
Institutions of old
Will they adapt, evolve
Or forever grow cold
Can they reclaim
Their purpose,

Their original intent
Or will they succumb
To the allure of wealth

Perhaps the answer lies
Not in the structures tall
But in the hearts
Of those
Who gather
One and all
For in the end
It's not the institution
That gives
But the connections
The love
The community
That lives.

As the world spins on
And empires rise and fall
These institutions
Must confront
Their purpose
Their call
To serve

To uplift
To bring hope
And peace of mind
Connect people
Or risk becoming relics
Of a bygone era
Left behind.

Quest

In quest of wonder
I wander free
A traveller's heart
That's meant to be,
Through mountains
Towering high and wide
I roam, a wanderer,
With heart full of pride.

I sail on rivers
Calm and deep
Canoeing, boating
My spirit does a leap
Rappelling down
With thrill and a scream
Climbing big trees
Channelling adventure's beam.

In tents, I reside
Under starry skies
Long walks,
I undertake,
With a twinkle
In my eyes,
Strangers met
Become friends
On the way
Together we travel
In a bond
That's here to stay.

Different cultures
I get to explore
A mosaic of traditions
Forever in store
I learn
I grow
With each new place
My heart, enriched
In a deeper sense

Travel, a bridge, that
Connects us all,
A bond that unites
Standing tall
In a country diverse
With cultures so bright,
Travel integrates,
Shining with delight.

So let us travel
Far and wide,
And in our journeys
May our hearts reside,
In the beauty of diversity
We'll find our way.

Innocent Souls

Innocent souls
With bodies worn
Genetic hands
That fate has sworn
Survival's quest
In a world unkind
Their story's told
In heart and mind.

Their parents' pain
A mental scar
A lifetime's journey
Near and far
The weight of worry
The stress and fear
A constant reminder
Always near.

Society's role
A responsibility true
To accept
To support
To see them through
No misplaced sympathy
No pitying stare
Just empathy
Understanding
And love to share.

Let's look beyond
The physical frame
And find the beauty
In their special name
Their abilities unique
Their strengths untold
A gift from God
A treasure to behold

Let's empower them
To stand tall and proud
Take care of themselves
In a world allowed

To protect them
From harm's way
And celebrate their
Differences in the light
Of day and night.

For they are special
In every single way
A blessing
A treasure
Here to stay
So let's cherish them
Love them just the same
And recognise the value
Of their unique flame.

The Journey We Made

Days of old
When radio
Was a marvel of sound
For me and you
Tape recorders amazed
With magnetic might,
A symphony of progress
To one's delight

TV and computers
Mere fantasies
Telephone lines scarce,
Connecting dreams
Mobile phones, a myth
A concept yet unknown,
Communication's journey
Long and cumbersome.

We adapted
Stage by stage
Through trials and strife
Witnessing wonders
Becoming part of life
The value of each innovation
We knew so well
The toil
The time
The struggles
The stories to tell.

But now
A new generation
With wonders
At their command
Take progress
For granted
With an expectant hand
They don't know
The struggles
The sweat
The tears
The hardships overcome
Through all the passing years.

They don't know
The waiting
The patience
The pain,
Of informing loved ones,
Of news that couldn't
Wait in vain
They don't know
The beauty
Of a simpler
Slower pace
The joy of connection
In a timeless
Sacred space.

But still we hold on
To memories of the past
A testament to progress Forever to last,
And though
The new generation
May not understand,
We'll cherish the journey
That made
Their world so grand.

Summer Woes

Oh moon so bright
Lighting up our night
Providing us delight
In this sweltering heat

But all for told
We will happily forgo
Your delightful presence
For rain clouds with summer shower
Lightning and thunder
For heat this summer
Has put us asunder

Summer's blaze,
A withering spell,

Dried the earth,
And all its dwell,
Water's scarcity,
A hardship to bear,
A precious resource,
Beyond compare.

The sun beats down,
Relentless and bright,
Draining life,
From the parched earth's sight,
Crops wither and die,
Without a reprieve,
A desolate landscape,
Our souls to grieve.

We yearn for rain,
A cooling, gentle breeze,
To soothe the earth,
And bring some relief,
To revive the plants,
And replenish the ground,
Quenching our thirst,
And turning the world around.

Friends

In life's journey
We meet many souls
Some stay awhile
While others make us whole,
Good friends are treasures
Rare and true
A bond that's nurtured
Forever shines through

A friend is not just one
Who's there for the fun,
But one who stands by you
When the journey's done,
When storms rage on,
And darkness falls near,
A true friend lends a hand,
And with you, he will stand

Fair-weather friends,
Who flee at the first sign,
Are not friends at all,
But mere acquaintances
Wealth, power and status
Should never come between,
For true friendship is pure
And forever serene.

A friend is one who sees
Beyond the facade
Who knows your heart,
And is not swayed,
By external trappings,
That can blind and deceive,
A true friend is a mirror,
That reflects and believes.

So let us nurture
These bonds so strong
And stand by each, a gift,
That's rare and divine
A treasure that's worth more
Than all one can imagine

Through life's ups and downs
Through every test of time
True friendship will endure,
And forever be sublime
So let us cherish these friends
Who stand by our side
With no strings attached
And honour the bond
That forever will abide.

A Marathon Run

Life's a marathon,
A long, winding road,
That tests our will,
Our strength,
Our soul's abode,
A journey that demands
Planning,
Pacing,
And might,
To conserve our energy,
And make it through the night.
Wealth is our fuel,
Our sustenance
For the future
To be managed wisely,
Lest we exhaust

A steady stride,
A consistent pace,
To avoid burnout,
And find a steady space.
Challenges arise,
Like hills and winding bends,
That push us to our limits,
And make our lungs burst,
But we must look inward,
To find the hidden reserve,
To draw upon our depths,
And let our spirit serve.
The limbs may tire,
The muscles may ache,
But the desire to finish,
Must our hearts not break,
For winning's not the goal,
But completion's the key,
To stand tall at the finish,
And proudly say, 'I've been'.
The coward's way,
Is to quit midway,
To abandon the journey,
And let fears have their say,
But we must face Obstacles,

With new-found courage
And plan our strategy,
To avoid imminent tragedy
Like a marathon runner,
We must face the grind,
With every step forward,
Leaving our doubts behind,
And when we finally cross,
The finish line's sacred space,
We'll know that we've
Conquered, life's marathon pace.

A Trek In Twilight

A journey of strangers,
United as one,
Through social media's thread,
Our trek had just begun,
Sixty souls, diverse ages,
From 18 to 65's prime,
I, a senior,
Fit and ready,
To take on the climb.
Anamudi's peak,
Our destination high,
The highest point in Kerala,
Touching the open sky,
The forest's initial stretch,
A gentle, easy pace,
But soon, the climb
Would challenge,

Every single face.
I found myself converse
Youngsters, half my age,
IT professionals from Bangalore,
With adventure's stage,
We clicked,
We connected,
Our spirits took flight,
Together we trekked,
Through golden light.
The forest's splendour,
Exhilarated our souls,
As we moved in sync,
Our bond began to unfold,
But when the climb intensified,
Struggles began to show,
Seniors coped better,
While youngsters faltered,
Don't you know!
The group's dynamics shifted,
As we helped
Each other through,
Strangers became
Teammates,
United, to see this

Journey anew,
Those ahead, waited,
To lend a helping hand,
A testament to trust,
Forged in the fire
Of this challenging land.
At last, we reached the top,
Oh, what a feeling divine,

Standing tall, surrounded
By breathtaking views,
Sublime,
The descent,
A different story,
But by now,
We were as one,
A well-oiled machine,
Moving in harmony,
Beneath the golden sun.
Our journey's end,
Marked the birth of lasting ties,
A brotherhood of strangers,
Bonded by trust,
And mutual surprise,
An experience etched,

In memory's
Sacred space,
To be repeated,
Relived,
And cherished,
With a smile on every face.

Together We Can

Deep in the ancient woods,
Where wisdom whispers low,
A treasure trove, of life,
For all to know,
Our forests stand,
As guardians of the earth,
A delicate balance,
Of nature's sacred birth.
But alas, we've ravaged,
With reckless, careless might,
A significant portion, lost
To the march of night,
The fauna and flora,
That once thrived with glee,
Now face extinction,
A tragedy, for you and me.

Countless species, gone
Forever, lost to our sight,
Others teetering,
On the brink,
Of endless nights,
The future generation,
Will hold us accountable,
For the destruction,
We've wrought,
In our own selfish way.

A road through the forest,
May ease travel's grind,
But widespread destruction,
Will soon be left behind,
Easy access,
For the unscrupulous,
And greedy of mind,
Will ravage the landscape,
Leaving devastation,
Hard to unwind.
So let us join hands,
To conserve,
To protect,
And to defend,

Our common forest wealth,
A treasure, that will never end,
Every small action counts,
Every voice matters,
Every hand needed
Together we can,
Make a difference,
Across this land.
For the forests are,
The lungs of our Earth,
Producing oxygen,
Giving life and rebirth,
They shelter,
They nourish,
They protect,
And they provide,
A treasure,
So precious,
We cannot,
Afford to divide.
So let us act now,
To preserve,
To conserve,
And to save,
Our forests,

Our future,
Our very existence,
We must crave,
For a better tomorrow,
We must strive, today,
To protect, to defend,
Our forests, come what may

Xmas – A Memory

In Kochi's streets,
Where Christmas magic's spun,
I yearn to be
Beneath the festive sun,
From December's start,
The vibe begins to shine,
A city aglow, with stars,
And festoons divine.
Broadway's bustling,
With shoppers galore,
Families flocking, to stores
Laden evermore,
Mather Street's ablaze,
With colourful delight,
Crowds seeking treasures
To make Christmas bright.
Oh, for a taste

Of Casino Padhal's cake,
Double-matured, a flavour,
My senses would partake,
And homemade wines,
Crafted with love and care,
A Christmas tradition,
Beyond compare.
Fort Kochi's enchantment,
Beckons me to roam,
A fairytale setting,
Where lights dance,
And magic's home,
The veli tree's splendour
A sight to behold,
The Christmas fair's excitement,
For young and old.
Casa Kitchen's Athazha Biriyani,
A late-night treat,
Lingers on my palate,
A flavour, hard to beat,
Koch's Christmas charm,
A nostalgia, so true,
Calling me back,
To experience it anew.
This Christmas, I'll hold,

These memories so dear,
Of Kochi's festive splendour,
And joy, that brings a tear,
Though far away,
My heart remains,
In this special place,
Kochi, my Christmas haven,
Where love and magic,
Fill the space.